WHAT'S IN THIS BOOK?

GW00570482

Please note:
- this book provides support and advice that is relevant for any child with SEND
- death in this book relates to any death that a child with SEND may experience: parent, sibling, family member, friend, peer, teacher, carer, support staff etc.
- when we refer to 'parents' or 'siblings' we include the rich variety of family relationships, for example, step–parents and half–siblings
- all information and guidance given in this book is applicable to any type of bereavement
- this book focuses on the needs of bereaved children with SEND but its guidance and support includes any bereaved child
- when we use the term child or children it includes children and young people with SEND
- there is a glossary of terms used in this book on page 68

GENERAL SUPPORT

The Elephant in the Room by Terry Kettering

There's an elephant in the room.
It is large and squatting, so it is hard to get around it.
Yet we squeeze by with 'How are you?' and 'I'm fine.'
And a thousand other forms of trivial chatter.
We talk about the weather.
We talk about work.
We talk about everything else...
except the elephant in the room.

There's an elephant in the room.
We all know it is there.
We are thinking about the elephant as we talk together.
It is constantly on our minds.
For you see, it is a very big elephant.
It has hurt us all.
But we do not talk about the elephant in the room.
Oh please, say her name.
Oh please, say 'Barbara' again.

Oh please, let's talk about the elephant in the room.
For if we talk about her death,
Perhaps we can talk about her life?
Can I say 'Barbara' to you and not have you look away?
For if I cannot, then you are leaving me
Alone...
In a room...
With an elephant...

First Year, Worst Year by B. WIlson & M. Wilson
Reproduced with permission from Wiley Global.

Death is a part of all our lives and most children will experience the death of someone they loved. Children with special educational needs and disabilities (from here on referred to as SEND) are no different. Often children with SEND are more likely to experience the death of someone close to them at a younger age and more often than their typically developing peers. This is due to the medical needs of some children with SEND, children with life–limiting or life–threatening issues. Children with SEND will have a whole range of friends, but often they will have friends who also have SEND, some of whom may have medical needs.

The needs of bereaved children with SEND can be overlooked or forgotten. This can be as a result of adults:

• not wanting to upset the child by talking to them about death

• feeling the child has enough to cope with already without having to deal with death too

These thoughts come from a place of love and care but they should not prevent us from talking openly and honestly with a bereaved child with SEND. Without support we are leaving the child 'alone in a room with an elephant'.

Other views that can result in a child with SEND not receiving bereavement support can be a belief that the child:

• is not old enough to understand

• does not have the cognitive ability to understand the loss

However, we understand that these beliefs are not accurate. A young baby acknowledges the loss of someone close to them, such as the absence of their touch, voice and smell. They also pick up on the changes in their environment (both practical and emotional changes). At the very least, children with SEND will be affected by the death of someone they were close to in the same way, with some bereaved children with SEND being affected in far greater ways. It all depends on the child's level of understanding (see page 8).

Another potential barrier to children with SEND not having their grief recognised and supported is the exact nature of the child's SEND e.g. delayed or impaired cognition, physical, sensory and/or emotional skills. However, these are in fact all barriers to bereavement support for us, as adults, to overcome – and we can. It is all about us having the confidence and skills to do so. Knowing the best language and modes of communication to use when talking about death. Understanding how to deliver and present the information, as well as having the most appropriate resources and activities to use. All of these are covered in this book.

THE INCLUSIVE NATURE OF GRIEF

UNDERSTANDING HOW CHILDREN WITH SEND GRIEVE

For a child with SEND, their functional level of understanding (rather than actual chronological age) will be the biggest factor in how the child reacts to a death and what they will be able to understand.

Knowing what children at different developmental stages understand about death will help you feel more confident when talking to them about a bereavement.

The information in the following pages outlines what children at different developmental levels:

• will understand

• what you may see (their responses and the behaviours they may exhibit)

• what you can do to help

Children with SEND can often have spiky developmental profiles and therefore do not always fit neatly into one box. The bereaved child you are supporting may display aspects of one or more of the developmental stages. Please bear this in mind as you read the following pages.

CHILDREN WITH SEND WHO ARE FUNCTIONING AT A 0-12 MONTHS LEVEL

What they understand

- The death of a parent/significant caregiver will be understood as the absence of the person who cared for them. They will acknowledge and miss the touch, sound, smell etc. of this person, but they will not understand why they have gone.

- Other deaths will be experienced by the child as a change in their environment. They will pick up on the emotions of the people around them who are grieving and the possible subsequent changes in their daily routines, although they will not understand why.

- They can feel strong emotions but they are unaware of what these are or what is causing them.

What you may notice

- Grief is expressed through loss of security and this may be seen in changes in their eating and sleeping habits.

- They may cry and generally appear less settled, more irritable and even inconsolable.

- They may become more clingy to the adults in their life.

- The child's emotions are expressed through their body language.

What may help

- Where possible, try to keep their routines the same as they were before the death. This will help them to feel safe and secure.

- The child will experience the world mainly through their senses and physical sensations, so try to surround them with familiar smells, textures, sounds, rhythms and tastes. This could be by giving them an item of clothing worn by the person who has died, which still bears their scent.

- Make sure they have easy access to all of the usual things that give them comfort: a weighted blanket, twiddle toy, musical instrument etc.

CHILDREN WITH SEND WHO ARE FUNCTIONING AT A 1 TO 3 YEAR OLD LEVEL

What they understand

- They may be aware that someone is missing, but will not fully understand why.
- They will not understand the finality of death and so may expect the person who has died to come back.
- They will notice the changes in their life caused by the death, particularly changes relating to their routines and care.
- They will react to other people's emotional state, which they may not understand.

What you may notice

- They may try to search for the person who has died.
- They will show their feelings through changes in behaviour and play.
- You may see some angry behaviour or emotional outbursts.
- They may become more withdrawn.
- You may notice more crying.
- They may become clingier towards key adults in their life.
- Their eating, sleeping and toileting habits may change and/or their skills in these areas may temporarily regress.
- They may become anxious in the company of strangers.

What may help

- Take their worries and questions seriously.
- Listen and help them feel that they are not alone.
- Try to keep their routines the same.
- Talk to them frequently about what has happened – in very simple terms.
- Pay attention to what the child is doing; their play and behaviours may give an insight into how they are feeling.
- Looking at simple picture books about death and loss together.

CHILDREN WITH SEND WHO ARE FUNCTIONING AT A 3 TO 5 YEAR OLD LEVEL

What they understand

• They will struggle to understand what dead means.

• They may expect the person who died to return.

• They will miss the person who has died.

• A child at the top end of this developmental level may understand some of the physical reasons behind a death but will still find this difficult to grasp.

• They may be able to recognise some feelings but are unlikely to be able to link it to their grief.

What you may notice

• They will listen to what adults are saying, even if they do not fully understand what it means.

• They may learn to use words associated with death without understanding them.

• They will take explanations literally.

• They may ask the same question time and time again.

• They may think that they did something to cause the death.

• Changes in behaviour and play as they act out their feelings.

• Increased anger, shown in emotional outbursts or shouting, often linked to anxiety.

• Increased fears and worries.

• They may experience difficulty separating from their parents or carers.

• Difficulty concentrating on activities.

• They may become withdrawn from friends and could find it more difficult to relax and enjoy themselves.

• Their eating, sleeping and toileting habits may change or regress temporarily.

• A child may develop physical symptoms like tummy aches and headaches.

• Some children may appear not to react much to the death at first.

What may help

• Love, comfort and reassurance to build a child's confidence and help them to feel safe again.

• Reassurance that they are cared for and knowing who will look after them.

• Explaining the death in simple, concrete terms that reflect their developmental stage.

• Maintaining routines and boundaries.

• Voicing emotions for them.

• Learning how it affects other people helps them to learn to express their own feelings and feel less alone, developing emotional literacy.

• Help the child remember the person who has died: by talking about them, looking at things that belonged to them etc.

• Participating in family rituals to say goodbye.

• Continuing to talk to them about what has happened.

CHILDREN WITH SEND WHO ARE FUNCTIONING AT A 6 TO 9 YEAR OLD LEVEL

What they understand

• They will be beginning to develop an understanding that death is irreversible.

• That death is something that will happen to all living things but they may still be confused about it and have many questions.

• It is not uncommon for children at this developmental level to think of death as something spooky, like a monster or a spirit that comes to get you.

What you may notice

• They may display what you feel is an overly strong interest in the physical aspects of death such as what a dead body looks like and what happens to a body after a person has been cremated.

• They may worry about how the person who has died will eat, breathe and keep warm.

• Children at this stage may complain of a sore tummy, headaches or of just generally not feeling well. These are what we call somatic complaints, where unexpressed feelings and emotions can lead to physical symptoms or discomfort.

• Children at this functional age may have difficulty expressing feelings verbally and may retreat into themselves. In dealing with their feelings of helplessness, you may notice increased aggression.

What may help

• Curiosity about death is natural and the child will benefit from clear explanations.

• It is important to give them information and tell them that once someone has died, the body doesn't feel pain any more, nor does it feel hot or cold or get hungry.

• It is important that their specific worries are spoken about, that they share bad dreams and are told that what they're feeling is normal.

• Children are reassured by having their worrying and negative thoughts talked through.

• Somatic complaints are normal but it is important that routines are maintained while gently acknowledging that it hurts when someone important dies.

• It is important to avoid clichés such as: 'You're such a brave boy/girl'. Children may interpret this to mean that you don't want them to share their feelings. They need you and other important people in their lives to show them that it is OK to express their feelings.

What they understand

- At this developmental level children are much more aware of the finality of death and the impact the death has on them.

- They are able to understand death as both concrete and abstract.

- Children at this stage are beginning to think of the longer–term consequences of the loss of the relationship.

- They are aware of the loss they feel in the present but also of the losses they will experience in the coming months and years. The child will begin to understand that there will be further grief in the future – as the person who has died will not be with them for important milestones or occasions.

What you may notice

- Children may experience difficulties in their interactions with their peers.

- The death of someone important can make them feel different when they desperately want to be the same as everyone else.

- At this developmental age children are beginning to move away from dependence on the family and they start to form important relationships with other children.

- Big emotional releases (such as anger or distress) are not uncommon but can be scary for children at this stage.

- Their ability to manage their feelings may be disrupted and can lead to mood swings or more definite ups and downs in their feelings.

- That the death of someone important can easily destabilise a child/young person.

What may help

- The child needs to know that they have the safety and security of their family.

- It is important to find ways to build their self–esteem.

- Your willingness to listen and your assurances that their feelings are normal.

- Finding ways to normalise their thoughts and feelings; this might include sensitively sharing your own experience and/or common feelings and thoughts of others who have been bereaved.

CHILDREN WITH SEND WHO ARE FUNCTIONING AT A 13+ YEAR OLD LEVEL

What they understand

• At this stage children will have a full understanding of death, the fact that it is permanent and that it is something that affects all living beings.

What you may notice

• They may withdraw and act very matter of fact and detached, or angry and protesting.

• They may be so busy with different activities that they don't stop to reflect. This can be an effective way of keeping intense feelings under wraps if they are worried about losing control of their emotions.

• That their friends and peers are very important and they will probably talk to them about the death rather than their family.

• They may be developing many of their own ideas and thoughts about the world and could challenge their family's beliefs and views on death.

• They may struggle to make longer–term plans as the death of someone important causes them to reflect on 'the meaning of life' and ponder on the question 'What's the point?'

• You may see some risk–taking behaviour at this stage as they test the boundaries.

What may help

• Remain open and available to them and let them know it is natural to have questions or thoughts that they need to come back to.

• Remind them of your continued love and support.

• Remind them that you are there for them but if they would prefer to speak to someone else that is OK. You can then help them find peers or other trusted adults to support them.

• To understand that they want to be accepted by other important people in their lives.

As well as a child's developmental level of understanding, there are other things that can impact a child's reaction to a death and therefore influence behaviours:

"When my sister died, my son was devastated. Aunty Carly was his second mum. She'd always been there helping to support him and me with his care." Kerry (mum of a 12 year old with cerebral palsy)

The level of attachment they had to the person who has died – the stronger the relationship the more likely it is for them to be affected.

"This was the first person that Zoe knew who had died. Our dog had died the previous year though and this helped us to start to talk about the death and what it meant." Jim (dad of a 7 year old with Down's syndrome)

Their prior experiences of illness, death and loss – previous experiences will help them to cope with the current one.

"She was elderly and had been ill for a long time. Rani knew this and had visited her in hospital. This helped her to understand things a little more easily." Meera (mum of a 14 year old with autism)

How the death occurred – long illness, accident, sudden death, suicide etc.

"We never talked about death and we aren't a religious family. When his grandfather died we had no idea where to start to try and explain things to him." Darren (dad of a 10 year old with severe learning difficulties)

The family's **cultural background** and **religious beliefs** – this will have an influence on how the child views death.

"It was wonderful that her Brownie leader took the time to talk about the bereavement with her and this encouraged her friends to talk to her about it too." Sophie (mum of an 8 year old with dyslexia)

The type and number of **support networks** the child has at home, school etc.

"Our children reacted so differently. Izzie shared every single thought and question. Patrick said nothing about it for weeks." Elly (mum of 11 year old twins with learning & physical disabilities)

The **gender** of the child – not always, but boys can be less likely to show their emotions.

We *all* experience grief.

We *all* need support with grief at times and this includes individuals with SEND.

How much more frightening is something if we don't understand what is going on?

The same is true for children with SEND.

LET'S TALK ABOUT DEATH

THE NATURE OF DEATH

As adults we can sometimes find certain deaths easier to cope with than others. An elderly relative dying due to old age after a long and happy life can be easier to come to terms with than your neighbour's little girl dying in a car accident. This is not about one person meaning more to you than another: It is about our thoughts on the natural order of life – we expect people to live long into retirement.

For children with SEND, the nature of a person's death can also be significant.

If the person died:

- as a result of **old age**, remind the child that they are still very young and that the person who has died lived all through their own childhood, getting a job, buying a house, getting married, etc. (whatever is relevant) and that the child still has all of this yet to do.

- in **hospital** and the child has to visit hospitals a lot, it is vital that we explain to them that not all people who visit hospitals die. Thousands of people visit a hospital every day and the vast majority are made better by the doctors and nurses.

- in a **car accident**, the child may become fearful of travelling in a car. As with the hospital scenario, explain the numbers of people who travel safely by car every day and that car accidents are rare.

- of the **same/similar condition or illness that the child has**, then this can be immensely worrying for the child. In this case, we need to be honest with the child, but also positive and optimistic. *'Yes, Charlie had the same condition as you, but remember each person's illness is different. Charlie has sadly died, but it doesn't mean you're going to die any time soon.'* If it is appropriate, you may also want to say something like *'doctors and scientists are coming up with new medicines and treatments all of the time to help improve things for people with (name of the child's condition)'*.

- as a result of **suicide**. It is important that we don't tell children lies or half–truths. We also shouldn't give them information that they do not understand. When the death is complex such as death by suicide, its often better to present the facts a bit at a time e.g. 'Mummy has died and it's really sad' and then add more detail later. Then use the jigsaw approach (as discussed on page 19) As the child's understanding develops, they may ask for more details about the nature of the death – provide them with these details at this point. Winston's Wish provide a guide to talking about suicide *Beyond the Rough Rock* and the experienced practitioners on our freephone helpline are always available to help think through how to talk about this, and any other issues.

TELLING A CHILD WITH SEND THAT SOMEONE HAS DIED

A key aspect to supporting bereaved children with SEND (and any bereaved child), is to be honest and open with them. This means we need to:

- **Tell them what has happened** e.g. *'Nanny has been very ill and the doctors and nurses have worked very hard to try and make her better, but sadly they were unable to'* – supplying details appropriate to the child's level of understanding.

- **Use the real words and no half–truths** when explaining to the child what has happened. Use the correct terms – dying, death and dead, rather than euphemisms such as 'passed away'. Using these accurate words makes it much clearer and easier for the child to understand. Avoid telling half–truths. If a child asks you a question, answer it honestly. If you answer with a lie you will only have to unpick it later and this is infinitely more difficult than just telling the truth in the beginning.

- **Answer the child's questions** immediately or if you are unsure of the answer, say *'I don't know, but I'll find out for you'*. Then find out the answer as quickly as possible and immediately share this with the child. However unusual or insignificant you may feel the question is, for the child it is immensely significant. Having the answer will help to reassure the child.

- **Accept their feelings**, even if these feelings are not as you thought they would be. Some children will react in a way that we find surprising, e.g. laughing when they learn that someone has died. This is not the child being rude, rather it is their immediate and emotional reaction. The news is so big it is the child's only way of coping with it.

- **Let them know that is is not their fault** – some children may worry that the person has died as a result of something they have or have not done. It is imperative that we explain to the child (to the level of their understanding) how and why the person died and that this was not caused by anything they did or said. It can be helpful to repeat this whenever the death is explained to them.

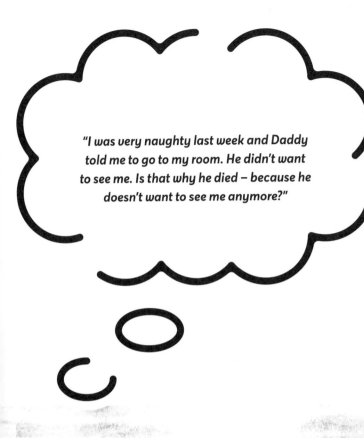

"I was very naughty last week and Daddy told me to go to my room. He didn't want to see me. Is that why he died – because he doesn't want to see me anymore?"

- **Deliver information about the death in small chunks** rather than giving the child lots of information all in one go. Instead, provide it gradually: a drip, drip approach of all of the relevant information.

- **Provide information about the death to their level of understanding.** As the child gets older and their understanding develops further, slowly give the child more information about how the person died. The types of questions that the child is asking will help to gauge their comprehension of the situation and how much information you should provide. It is like giving a new version of a jigsaw puzzle with more pieces in it. The earlier simpler jigsaw still gave a clear picture, for instance, *'Daddy has died and cannot come back to life'*. Later a child may be able to understand and assimilate other pieces of information that give a more detailed picture of how he died and factors that may have contributed to his death. The complexity of the picture and the number of pieces of information that a child can make sense of will be determined by their level of understanding.

- **Ensure the child trusts you** – regularly remind the child that you will always listen and that they can ask questions and share their thoughts and feelings with you at anytime.

- **Are you sitting comfortably?** When you share the news of the death, think about where you do this and how – the physical environment and positioning of you and the child. Choose a place that is relaxing and comfortable for the child. Sit alongside the child, rather than standing over them. Be ready to provide comfort. For some children it may not be appropriate to be seated face to face as this puts too much focus on them. Instead, they may prefer no direct eye contact. If this is the case, you can talk to them about the death by being 'side by side', perhaps looking at a shared view, or walking together. This approach will be much less challenging for them.

- **Reiterating the news**. You may need to deliver the news of the death and information concerning the loss many times before the child truly digests it and is able to understand that the person is not coming back. This may be difficult if you too are grieving. If this is the case try to have a few people (who are close to the bereaved child) available to reiterate the news of the death and answer the child's questions. This will help lessen the emotional impact on you.

- **Give the child enough processing time**. When talking to the child make sure you allow enough time between each sentence. This allows the child to process what they are being told. We generally underestimate the amount of processing time that a child with SEND requires. Don't be afraid of these processing silences – they will feel longer to you than they actually are.

- Try to **speak at a similar speed and level as the child**. Mirroring the way the child speaks not only comforts them, it also helps to ensure understanding. The speed at which the child speaks will often be similar to the speed at which they process the information you are providing.

- **Echo** back to the child anything that they say and share with you, but in a slightly different way. This 'echo' not only reinforces that you have listened to them and that you care, but the repetition also helps them to further understand the loss.

- **Do not rely merely on words.** Ensure you deliver information about the death to the child using the child's preferred mode(s) of communication e.g. sign language, symbols, PODD book etc. Even if the child has verbal language, it is best to support conversations with Augmentative and Alternative Communication (AAC) such as symbols, photos, sign language, etc. When presented with difficult news, our emotions become heightened and our skills can diminish. Having the information presented in a range of different ways makes it easier for the child to follow and understand. (For further information about AAC see page 27.)

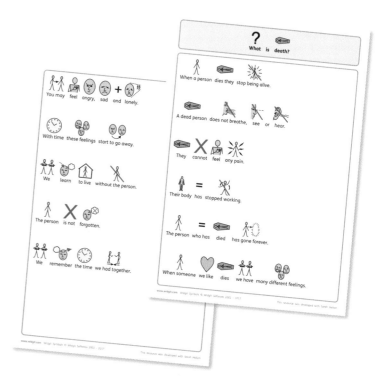

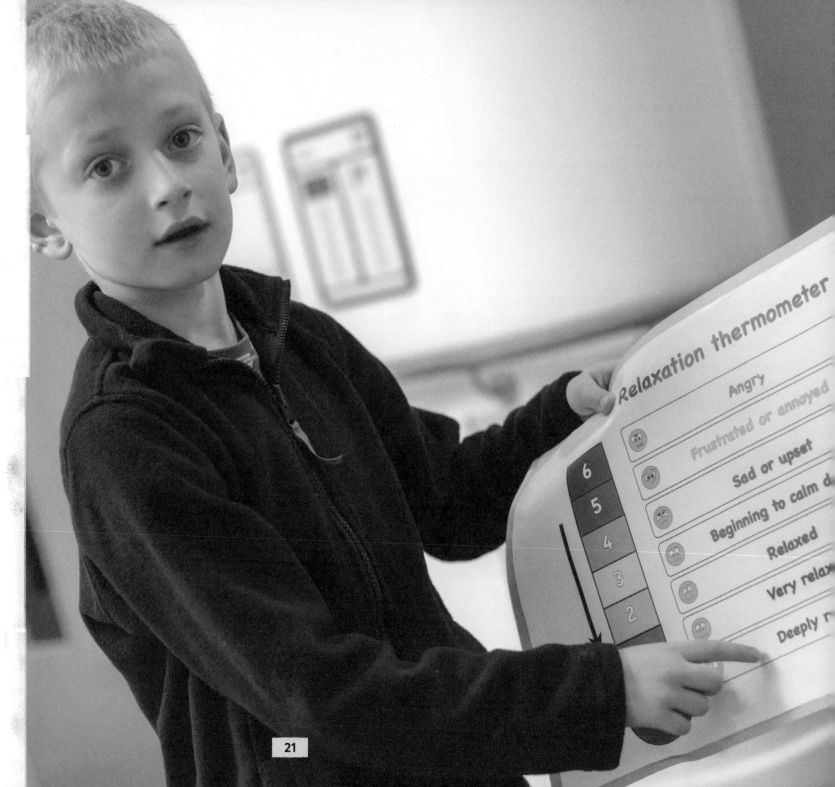

- **Ensure that the child can express their thoughts and feelings.** This means having the appropriate AAC (see page 27) and other resources prepared and available for the child to use. At the very least, have a photo of the person who has died accessible to the child so that they can look at it and also so they can present it to you when they want to talk about the person who has died or share their feelings.

21

There are four main aspects to grieving though they are not neat and sequential. We move in and out of each of them many times, with things sometimes getting harder before they start to improve.

A bereaved child with SEND will be the same and we need to support and guide them with these aspects of grieving.

- **Coming to terms with the death and accepting that it has happened.** We will need to share the news of the death and explain what this means to them many times.

> The child's father has died and he's worried that he will no longer be able to attend his football club as Dad was the person that always took him.
> *"I know you're sad that Daddy has died and you're worried that you won't be able to go to football now but don't worry. You will still go every Saturday morning – Uncle Mike is going to take you."*

- **Adjusting to a world where the person is no more.** We will need to support the child with how to live in a slightly different world, a world without their loved one.

> The child's mother has died.
> *"I know it's strange in the house without Mum. There are so many things that remind us of her – things like the purple mixer that she loved and the two of you made amazing cakes with. I know it will be hard at first, but we can still make those great cakes – you and I can make them together and we can remember how Mum always found it funny that I never wear an apron when I cook, even though I make such a mess!"*

- **Living through the physical and emotional effects of the loss.** We will need to help the child manage the practical changes in their life and the range of emotions they are experiencing.

> A bereaved child experiencing headaches.
> *"When someone dies we can sometimes forget to do the usual everyday things like eating and looking after ourselves as we are busy thinking about the person who has died. It is very sad that your friend Lucy has died and I know you're thinking about her a lot. You're holding your head because it hurts – that's probably because of all the feelings and emotions going on in your body. It might help if we have a walk to the park – we can get some fresh air and remember how Lucy loved to spin on the swing."*

- **Finding ways to remember the person.** We will need to work with the child to build and store memories of the person who has died.

> The family cat has died and the child was very close to it – they had known the cat their entire life.
> *"We all miss Betty so much. She was a great cat, she really loved you and liked to look after you. Whenever we couldn't find Betty she'd be on your bed! Shall we choose a photo of Betty and get it made into a cushion so that you can have it on your bed to cuddle and remember her?"*

Bereavement isn't a linear process. The emotions of grieving are wide–ranging and in no way constant. They can change in a single moment. Think of your own experiences of loss – one minute you can be distraught with emotion, crying or angry and then you remember something silly that the deceased person did and you can be overcome with laughter.

All children (regardless of their ability) who are experiencing a bereavement will dip in and out of their grief. We cannot always predict how or when they will be affected.

Listening and showing that you care are the key aspects of supporting a bereaved child with SEND.

23

SUPPORTING A BEREAVED CHILD WHO HAS AUTISM

There are many stereotypes as to what a person with autism 'looks like', 'acts like' 'understands' and 'feels'. **All children are individuals – all children with autism are individuals.** Therefore we cannot provide one scenario of what a bereaved child will 'look like' or one way we should help them when they are grieving. The same applies to a bereaved child with autism. Instead, below is a range of things to consider when supporting a bereaved child who has autism.

- **Acknowledge their grief.** Just because the child may not respond to a death in a way we expect or that is similar to how other children react does not mean that they are not grieving.

- **Are they affected by the death?** You may be unsure as to how much the child is affected by a person dying. Think about how the child behaves on a typical day and then assess how far they are deviating from their 'norm'. Most people who receive bad news will behave a little differently, so we should not be overly concerned when a child with autism does this too. If the child's reaction involves them becoming angrier and more physical, we need to ensure that they are safe by removing dangerous objects etc. Wait until this physical emotion has passed and then talk to the child using AAC (see page 27) about the person who has died and how it is affecting the child.

- Use **very concrete language** when talking about the death. Euphemisms such as 'they are no longer with us' will cause a great deal of confusion to children with autism. They may interpret this as 'the person is no longer living with us, they are living with someone else, so we may get to see them again in the future.'

- Many children with autism spectrum disorder (ASD) benefit from the use of **social stories or comic strip conversations** to help them understand new information or situations. A social story is a short description of an event or situation and the text is often supported with pictures, photos and/or symbols. A comic strip conversation is made up of simple drawings and stick figures which accompany the information. Colour can be added to the words in the comic strip to help represent the emotional content of the statements.

• Be prepared that a bereaved child with autism may become **more impulsive** in their behaviour and reactions. Such changes might indicate that they require an even greater level of support to help understand what has happened and why their life has changed in certain ways.

> *The child may typically seek opportunities for sensory stimulation from spinning objects and looking at their movement, but following the bereavement they may take this to a new and dangerous level e.g. climbing onto high furniture to spin both the objects and themselves.*

• Some children with autism may struggle to see how the death is impacting others. They themselves may not be too affected by the bereavement but others around may be, which they cannot understand. This may result in them appearing insensitive to others.

> *A pupil in the school has died but because it wasn't someone they knew they aren't sad about the loss and they don't understand why other children are upset and crying.*

• **Tough questions**. You may be asked some difficult questions or some that you do not see as important. For example *'What temperature is the fire at the crematorium?'* To an unprepared person this could be a very upsetting question. Remember, for the child, this question equals a concern. An unanswered question or concern will lead to anxiety and distress. If you do not know the answer to the question, tell the child you will find out for them and then do so as quickly as possible. If the child has numerous 'tough questions' that are all being directed to one person (who is finding it upsetting), find someone who is comfortable answering such queries and ensure the child knows they can go to them with these questions.

• The child's **preoccupations,** if they have any (such as reciting lines from favourite cartoons, spinning small objects, playing with water etc.) may increase in intensity following a bereavement or they may develop new preoccupations. Children with autism tend to dislike changes to their routines and a death in the family will typically result in many changes occurring. This can lead to the child's anxiety levels rising. To help lower their anxieties, keep explaining (using the child's preferred mode of communication) what has happened and that the death is not their fault (see page 17).

• After someone has died there are many **rituals** that can take place. The child will probably never have experienced most of these before, such as dressing up to go to a big building that echoes and having to sit still on a very hard pew. Such things can seem strange and bewildering. Talk to the child about such events and rituals in advance of them taking place and, if possible, support this with a social story (for further information see page 24) and having practice runs, e.g. visiting the church before the funeral etc.

• A child with autism may experience **sensory difficulties** (issues with smells, sounds, textures, light etc.). There can be many sensory elements associated with funerals – wearing restrictive formal clothes to a memorial service, the scent of flowers, the feeling of sitting on hard seats and immovable pews. If your child experiences such sensory difficulties, try to:

  • **alleviate** as many of these as possible (e.g. do they have to wear a shirt and tie to the service?)

  • **adapt** to the situation (e.g. take their favourite cushion and blanket to the church for them to sit on)

  • **prepare** them for the differences that are going to occur with social stories, trials of the sensory issue (e.g. practise wearing different shoes) and visits (to the new environment they will be visiting)

SUPPORTING A BEREAVED CHILD WHO HAS COMMUNICATION AND LANGUAGE DIFFICULTIES

For children who are pre–verbal, non–verbal or have limited language, it is crucial that a wide range of AAC techniques and tools are employed when talking to them about death, bereavement and grief.

Note: Verbal language and cognitive understanding are two very separate things. A child may be unable to vocalise their thoughts through verbal words but this does not necessarily mean they do not understand at a typical level. We must always remember the cognitive level of understanding of the bereaved child and speak to them at this level. Do not just see the physical disability and assume that all areas of the child's life are functioning in this way. Each child is an individual. For children with a good understanding of language, but non–standard means of 'speaking' to us, we must remember to speak to them at the level of their understanding, using their preferred mode of communication (e.g. sign language, communication aid, eye gaze, etc.).

This particular section is focused on children who have learning difficulties and difficulties producing verbal language. For these children there are many different communication techniques, strategies, resources and pieces of equipment that we can use to help when sharing the news of the death, answering their questions or concerns, as well as providing good ongoing support.

SUPPORTING A CHILD'S UNDERSTANDING OF DEATH USING AUGMENTATIVE AND ALTERNATIVE COMMUNICATION (AAC)

There are many different types of AAC:

No-tech: does not require anything beyond the user's body

Low-tech: involve something external to the user that may be non-electronic or a simple electronic device

High-tech: electronic devices similar to computers

NO-TECH AAC

Body language, gestures, eye-pointing, facial expression.

Sign language There are many different sign language systems (Makaton, Signalong, British Sign Language, etc).

Intensive Interaction Takes place when a child and an adult sit (or whatever position is most comfortable for the child) closely together and the adult copies whatever noise and/or movement the child makes. The child quickly sees that they are making something happen. Whenever they do something, it is copied; they are in control of the interaction. This repetition and reinforcement of their sounds and movements, the back and forth of the exchange, is a conversation. The power of using Intensive Interaction with bereaved children is that it clearly shows the child that the adult is listening to them. When Intensive

Interaction is an integral part of a child's learning programme, it not only helps them to develop early language skills, it also gives them greater confidence and empowers them to express their emotions and feelings. Following a bereavement, the grieving child may make some different sounds. This is a way of them releasing their emotions. When the adult copies the child's more guttural, sad sounds, the child sees they have been listened to and that they are not the only person feeling the way they do.

Non-verbal communication, such as Intensive Interaction, provides the bereaved child with another means to help cope with an overwhelming situation.

"Jenny always enjoys Intensive Interaction sessions, but after her brother died I noticed that the sessions were even more important to her. I had been caught up in planning the funeral and didn't give her as much attention as I should have. One morning she was rocking and banging her wheelchair. She wasn't crying but I could tell she wasn't feeling good. I went and sat by her and started to copy her actions and sounds. Within five minutes her body seemed to relax and her movements and sounds were happier." Lou (foster mum of an 18 year old with PMLD)

Photographs of the person who has died are essential. Ideally, this would be a collection of photos you can use when you are talking to the child so that they know exactly who you are referring to. This ensures there is no confusion for the child about who has died. After you have informed the child of the death, have the photos easily accessible to the child. This allows them to use a photo to tell you when they want to chat about the person, e.g. by bringing a photo to you, pointing to it or looking at the photo. A constantly accessible collection or book of photos is also good for the child because it gives them the ability to look through the images. This activity can be comforting for them, helping them to think about the person as well as the information they have been given and, in turn, process the loss.

Objects of reference are items typically used to represent an activity (e.g. a toy car to communicate 'We're getting in the car and going somewhere', a spoon to say, 'It's time to eat'). They can also represent a place (e.g. a piece of soap for the bathroom, a plastic flower for the garden). Objects of reference can be used to support bereavement and grief by having an item that can be used alongside the photo of the person. For example, if the person who died loved scarves and tended to wear them a lot, you may use one of their scarves when talking to the child. This object not only helps to make the child aware of who we are talking about, but the fact that it belonged to the person who has died means that it can also be a reassuring and comforting item – a tactile item for them to touch and explore.

Images and other photos such as pictures of a coffin, hearse, the crematorium, etc. help the child prepare for what they will be doing. It is also helpful to provide graphics showing different emotions that the child can look at, explore and use when they are struggling with how to express what they are feeling.

Switches are simple battery operated devices that allow you to record a single word or short message. The child then activates the message by pressing down on top of the switch. Switches come in a range of formats, single, double etc. When a child is bereaved, they may like to have a switch to say when they are feeling sad, or want to talk about the person who has died.

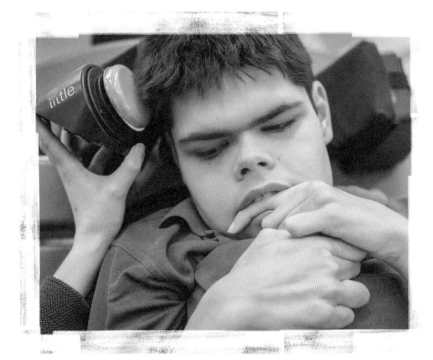

28

- **Symbols**. There are many different **symbol systems** (Boardmaker, Widgit, Makaton, etc.) Symbols are graphic representations of words. Symbols help to explain information, a concept, request, question, etc. to the child. The child will also use the symbols to share information, thoughts, questions, etc. with the adult. Some children will be working at a single symbol level, while others will be able to put symbols together to create sentences.

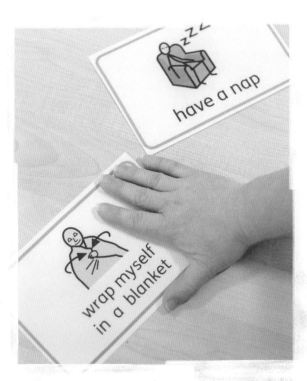

- **PECS** is a symbol–based communication system which allows children to develop a functional means of communication. A bereaved child who is a proficient PECS user will be able to express how they are feeling in simple terms (e.g. 'I feel sad', 'I want a hug').

- **PODD (Pragmatic Organisation Dynamic Display)** books are another symbol–based communication system, a resource that both the child and adult use to communicate with each other. The bereaved child can use the PODD book to point to symbols to express how they are feeling as well as to ask a question. There is a universal structure and layout to PODD books and it is a means of organising whole word and symbol vocabulary in one place. PODD books can be physical books or in an electronic form that children use on a tablet or via eye gaze technology.

29

- **Communication aids** are devices that have been made purely for the means of communication. The child selects the words that they wish to say and then the device 'speaks' these words.

- **Tablets**. There are various communication apps that can be loaded onto electronic tablets. The child chooses the words (which are commonly supported with a symbol) to say what they think, want, feel, etc. and the tablet then 'speaks' these words.

- **Eye gaze** is a way of accessing a computer using just your eyes. The equipment tracks the movement of the child's eyes, allowing their eyes to be the mouse and therefore the means of controlling the computer. Eye gaze can be used in conjunction with many computer programmes including communication software, enabling the child to express themselves, ask questions, etc. by using their eyes.

Whichever mode of AAC your child is using it is imperative to check that all of the relevant vocabulary is included. For example the word crematorium may not be included in the 'Places' section of the child's PODD book. The app on a communication device may not have all of the words necessary for the child to be able to 'tell the story' of the death and to allow them to ask questions about the bereavement. Ensure you add all appropriate vocabulary to communication aids and teach this new vocabulary to the child.

Whether it is high, low or no-tech the important thing is that it is always available to the child. How can they express how they are feeling if they do not have their 'voice' with them?

SUPPORTING A BEREAVED CHILD WHO HAS PROFOUND AND MULTIPLE LEARNING DIFFICULTIES (PMLD)

Children who have PMLD can face many extra barriers to receiving good bereavement support: for example, physical barriers such as wheelchairs, postural aids, medical equipment, etc.

Most children who are upset will want to be comforted, which involves closeness and physical contact. Make sure the equipment that children with PMLD require does not become a barrier to them receiving comfort.

How can you do this?

• When talking to the child about the person who has died, make sure that they have time out of all of the equipment. When we are feeling emotional, our bodies and breathing can become very tense. This will be the same for a child with PMLD. By being out of the wheelchair, they are able to have some freedom to release their tensions and emotions.

• Make use of the power of touch: touch equals 'I'm here for you, I'm listening, I care'. Even if the child is in their wheelchair you can still provide comfort through positive touch: a hand on their shoulder if they are sad, removing their shoes and socks and giving them a foot massage if they are distressed, etc.

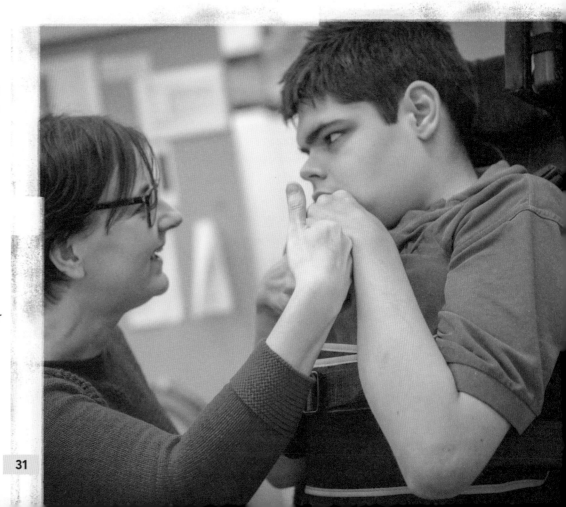

If a child has limited communication skills, are they grieving? YES! Remember – when a baby's main caregiver dies, the baby picks up on the changes in its life. They will notice that the smell, touch and feel of the person caring for them is different. The baby is attuned to differences in the atmosphere and mood of the home and the people around it (see page 5). Children with PMLD will (at the very least) be experiencing this, so we must talk to them about what is going on, supported by their preferred mode of communication (see page 27).

Talking helps us to deal with a bereavement.

While using AAC that the child is familiar with, talk to them about the person who has died. Not only explain in simple terms that the person has died and they will not be coming back, but also share memories (that involved the child) about the person.

Intensive Interaction is a great device for supporting bereaved children with PMLD as it supports them to express themselves and release their emotions. Massage and aromatherapy are two other good ways as they both encourage the child's body to relax and release their feelings.

Using the arts to support bereaved children. Music, art and dance are all excellent ways to support bereaved children with PMLD (see page 60).

The **power of breathing.** You may not be able to teach a child with PMLD how to do a three–part yogic breath but we can encourage them to breathe more deeply and fully. The easiest way to do this is to sit close to the child, relax and breathe deeply and slowly yourself. Given enough time, we tend to naturally mirror the breathing rhythm of the person we are with. If you slightly emphasise your breathing, this will make it a little easier for the child to pick up the deeper breathing technique. You can also, if the child is happy to do so, place their hand on your stomach so that they can feel it expanding as you breathe in and contracting as you breathe out. If the child is happy for you to do so, you can then place your hand on their stomach to encourage them to do the same.

WHAT FAMILIES WANT TO KNOW

SUPPORT FOR FAMILIES COPING WITH LOSS

Dealing with a bereavement is difficult for any family but when the family has a child with SEND, this may add an extra layer of concern.

If you have experienced this situation, you will probably have a range of thoughts and questions running through your mind:

Should you tell your child about the death?

How do you explain death to a child with SEND?

Where do you start?

How do you manage your own grief alongside supporting your child with their grief?

IT IS IMPORTANT TO ACKNOWLEDGE THAT THE DEATH WILL HAVE AN IMPACT ON YOUR CHILD

The level of impact the death will have on your child depends on the relationship they had with the person. If your child was very close to the person who has died they will, of course, have lots of questions and concerns. If the person who died was a friend of yours and not someone your child knew particularly well, you may be tempted to think that they will not be affected. This may be the case but your child will still pick up on your emotions and they will need to have an understanding of why you are sad and possibly behaving differently.

Families are a tight-knit community: what impacts one person will, to some extent, affect the whole family, because the emotions of one person will be seen and felt by everyone in the household, including a child with SEND.

MANAGING YOUR OWN GRIEF

Before looking at how you can support your child with their grief, let's first consider your own grief. It is important to remember that there is not one right way to cope. People react differently to a bereavement. How someone responds is unique and personal to them and can be affected by a range of factors: past experiences, personality, coping style, cultural background, level of support networks, religious and spiritual beliefs.

It is quite common for family members to respond differently to a death and at different times. Often members of a family try to protect each other: when one person is outwardly struggling with the loss, another will try to support them by being upbeat and positive. Although this is very normal, it can sometimes make it difficult for a family to be honest and open about their grief as they are fearful of upsetting each other.

You will be best placed to support your child with their grief if you first look after yourself. You will probably find it an enormous task to look after their needs and support them with their grief if you neglect your own physical and emotional self. At times this may seem daunting. You may find that friends and family are available to provide you with help and support. Sometimes it may be useful to talk to someone outside of your family and friends: a conversation with a neutral person such as a doctor or a call to the Winston's Wish Freephone National Helpline to get advice and guidance (see page 75).

Giving yourself time and space to process your thoughts and feelings is not an indulgence, it is an important part of the grieving process.

Communication is important for a family coping with loss. Make sure your child knows what has happened (to their level of understanding as explained in an earlier section) and how it impacts them.

HOW TO SHARE THE NEWS

As adults we are naturally inclined to protect and shield children from difficult and sad situations. We understandably find it very hard to see a child upset, especially if it is our own child. However, death is the one thing that we cannot change for children.

Some people may try to put off telling their child with SEND about a death. Delaying this conversation may initially alleviate their anxieties about having to share this difficult news, but in reality it is better to have the conversation sooner rather than later.

By giving children with SEND (as with all children) the facts about the death, we are helping them understand what has happened and supporting them with any changes this may bring about, which is best for the whole family.

PREPARATION AND PLANNING FOR THAT DIFFICULT CONVERSATION

Most conversations we have with our children take place naturally and without preparation and planning. When you have to talk to your child about a difficult subject, such as death, a little bit of preparation and planning will help you both.

Prior to sitting down with your child and telling them about the person who has died, take some time to think about what it is you want to say and how you can best present this information. This may mean preparing some symbols, adding extra words and phrases to their communication aid, or perhaps creating a social story or comic strip conversation of what has happened. Use whichever means of communication is most appropriate and engaging to your child.

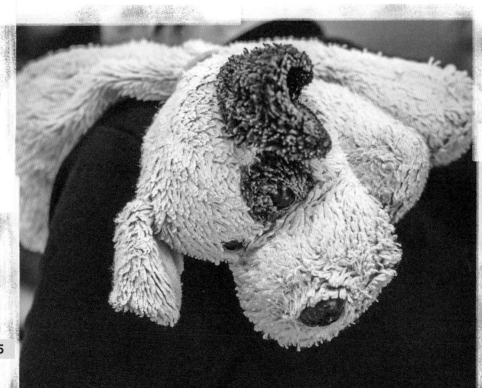

Sharing the news of a death needs to be done sensitively and honestly. Provide all of the relevant details to the level of your child's understanding using their preferred mode(s) of communication.

THE LANGUAGE OF LOSS

You need to ensure you have the means to communicate the following words and concepts (as appropriate to your situation):

- **dead**
- **alive**
- **will not see them again**
- **sad**
- **angry**
- **upset**

Along with words that explain how and where they died, such as:

- **very, very unwell**
- **accident**
- **in hospital**
- **at home**

> *Remember to avoid using euphemisms such as 'gone to a better place'.*

Once you have come up with the words and resources to explain what has happened, choose the best time (sooner rather than later) and place to have the conversation with your child.

This needs to be somewhere your child feels comfortable and relaxed, which will probably be in your home. Make sure your child is able to focus on what you have to tell them by ensuring they are not hungry, thirsty or about to do something. If they are about to go on a trip to the cinema or they are desperate for their lunch, they are not going to be able to focus on what you have to say.

An example of what to say when someone has died.

"James, do you remember that Aunty Tracy was in hospital because she was very ill? I'm afraid I have some sad news for you. The doctors couldn't make Aunty Tracy better and this morning her heart stopped working and she died."

An example of how to explain death.

"When a person dies they stop living. A dead person does not breathe, see or hear. They cannot do things. Their body has completely stopped working. They do not feel pain, or heat or cold, or get hungry. The person who has died has gone forever."

An example of how to explain grief.

"When someone we like dies, we can have many different feelings. We can feel angry, sad and lonely. With time these feelings start to get a bit better. We are able to learn to live without the person. The person is not forgotten. We remember them and the time we spent together."

TRY NOT TO SUPPRESS YOUR CHILD'S GRIEF

It can be hard seeing your child cry but tears are a way of releasing our emotions. If your child gets upset and starts to cry, comfort them and let them know it's OK to share how they are feeling. Be prepared to accept and support their feelings however they present them: tears, angry outbursts, silence etc.

Children learn how to walk, talk and share by observing others and through trial and error. The same applies to learning how to manage their emotions – they need to see it and explore it. As a family try to model 'how to grieve' to your child and teach them about the emotions of grief. By teaching your child these key skills you are also showing that you too are affected by the loss and that it is OK to grieve.

Be a good grief role model.

SEPARATION ANXIETY

Following a bereavement, it is quite normal for children to be worried about being apart from their parents. The death of someone close to them has rocked their world – normality has changed. They may try to reassure themselves and keep everything else the same by remaining close to family members. They may become clingy and unwilling to separate from you to go to school or even cry when you leave the room. It can be very hard to see a child upset in this way. Try to be patient and understand that with time and reassurance this period will pass. Give your child lots of affection and explain to them where you are going and when you will be back. Use your child's preferred modes of communication and AAC (as described on page 27) to support this information. Remember, even if your child has good receptive and expressive skills, at times of emotional distress the use of AAC alongside your words will help to explain things. They allow you to get the information across more easily and will aid the child's understanding.

HELP THE CHILD TO MANAGE THE CHANGE

Help the child to understand what death means and how it affects them and their emotions.

This will mean explaining what will and will not change as a result of the death (see the examples on page 22).

IS MY CHILD REACTING IN THE RIGHT WAY?

We tend to think that death = grief = sadness = tears but grief can look and feel totally different for each of us, including children with SEND.

Your child may **appear to be unaffected** by death. They carry on with life as before, following their typical routines and doing their usual activities. Just because a child does not outwardly display emotions of grief does not mean they have not acknowledged the absence of the person. In this situation, keep gently reiterating the information of the death alongside sharing your own emotions and memories of the person who has died. This ensures your child is building an understanding of what has happened and sees that it is OK to talk about the person who has died and how it is making them feel.

Some children may look as if they are **easily turning their feelings on and off.** Again, this does not mean that they are 'over the death'. Instead (like many adults), the child is able to grieve for the person who has died and also carry on with many aspects of typical life. They are learning to navigate between grieving and starting to move forward with their 'new normal' – life without that person.

A child can move in and out of their thoughts and feelings about a person dying very quickly. We may see them happily playing in the garden and then be inconsolable for no obvious reason. Or one minute they are angry and challenging you about why the person had to die and then they switch to wanting to know what they are having for tea.

You may feel that your child is **reacting more** than they should, as they were not that close to the person who has died. We can never predict how much a person will be affected. Your child may have thought more of the person that died than you realised or the impact that the death is having on the family as a whole could be what is unsettling your child.

COPING WITH DIFFICULT BEHAVIOURS

If your child is having to cope with the death of someone very close to them and they are struggling with this, they may exhibit some challenging behaviour. It is especially hard for children with communication difficulties to express how they are feeling. Their behaviour may be the only way they can express their grief.

These behaviours may range from being quiet and distant to temperamental, disruptive and aggressive. For some children this may include very challenging physical behaviour.

Children who exhibit challenging behaviour need to express their emotions, but it is our role to make sure that they do not hurt themselves or others. When your child is calm and receptive to your support, you can then talk to them about their grief and support their thoughts and understanding with more positive physical outlets.

> Some positive ways to physically express anger and frustration:
> - **throwing balls at a target**
> - **running**
> - **stomping on Bubblewrap**
> - **doing a large splatter painting**
> - **blowing up paper bags and popping them**
> - **climbing**

Being withdrawn is a behaviour that can so often be overlooked, especially if your child is without verbal language or does not have a very gregarious nature. Being withdrawn does not cause others a challenge, like a physical behaviour can, so it can easily go unrecognised. For a child with PMLD, or a child who is normally more engaged, it can be a very strong sign that they are struggling with their grief.

Following a bereavement, some children can become overly concerned about death and illness. They may spend a lot of time thinking about whether they are now going to die or whether their family and friends are going to die. If your child becomes worried in this way, you will need to reassure them that just because one person they know has died, it does not mean everyone around them will now suddenly die.

Other less common behaviours that children may exhibit are:

- **Talking to the person who has died or talking about them in the present tense.**

- **Imitating the person that has died: their speech, mannerisms, gestures etc.**

- **Starting to idolise the person who has died.**

As with any new behaviours a child may display, these need to be monitored. If you feel your child's behaviours are escalating or continuing for too long (in spite of the support you are giving them), you will need to seek further support and advice (see page 66).

DO NOT WORRY IF YOU SEE SOME REGRESSION

It is not uncommon for the skills of children to regress or stall after a significant event in their life. A death in the family is certainly one of these events. Following a bereavement, a child who had mastered using the toilet may start having accidents. Or a child who was using symbols to communicate stops doing so. Such regressions are due to your child's energy and focus being directed to trying to process their loss and understand what is happening. With time, love and patience your child's skills will return.

DIFFICULTIES WITH EATING AND SLEEPING

When we are in an emotional state, often the first things to be affected are our sleeping and eating habits. This can be the same for a grieving child. As a parent, it is natural to be concerned if your child is not eating as much as they usually would or their sleeping has become erratic. Keep an eye on these changes but do not panic. Typically these things will revert to their normal patterns given time and the child having the opportunity to talk about their worries and concerns with you.

BE PREPARED FOR YOUR CHILD'S GRIEF TO BE EXPRESSED AT ANY TIME

There is no standard timescale for grief. Your child may initially seem to be OK and then weeks or months later the impact of the bereavement hits them. For children with SEND this may not be shown through a clear expression of feelings but instead you may see a change in their eating or sleeping habits, or their behaviour becomes more difficult to manage. These can all be clues to their emotional state. Due to the unpredictable nature of grief, you may feel unprepared to support your child. Revisit your explanation of what has happened and why to your child (see page 18) using their preferred mode of communication (see page 26) and remind them that they can talk about the death and how it is affecting them at any time.

GRADUALLY BUILD UNDERSTANDING: NO LIES OR HALF-TRUTHS

If the circumstances of the death were difficult (e.g. suicide, a traumatic accident etc.), gradually build up the amount of information you give your child. As they ask for more information, you can add layers of detail to the story of the death. Winston's Wish provide a guide to talking about suicide, *Beyond the Rough Rock*, and the experienced practitioners on our freephone helpline are always available to help think through how to talk about this, and any other issues.

Children trust adults to tell them the truth, even if that is just a little bit at a time. If we give a child a fictitious or more palatable version of how the death occurred this may initially feel easier to manage but with time, your child will ask questions and seek out the truth. Having to unpick inaccurate information is far more difficult than giving the child the truth in bite–size pieces.

> *Gradually build up the layers of the story.*

ANSWERING DIFFICULT QUESTIONS

Some children may want a lot of detail about the death and they will have a great number of questions for you. Some of these you may not be prepared for or may shock you, questions such as *'How long will it take for the body to turn into a skeleton'*. The child is not asking these types of questions because they are being morbid or macabre. They are being curious about death and developing their understanding of what it means to die. Having answers to their difficult questions will help them to cope with the loss.

> *Unanswered questions can equal anxiety.*

If you do not know the answer to a question tell the child *'I don't know the answer to that question, but I will find out for you'*. Then find out the answer as quickly as possible and share it with the child.

Another strategy that may be appropriate is to give the child a visual reminder that they have an unanswered question that is being looked into for them, e.g. a card with a big question mark on it, or a symbol showing 'thinking'. This visual reminder will hopefully reassure the child that they are being listened to and will lower their concerns while the answer is being sought out. When you give the child the answer take the visual reminder away, which is then available for future use.

If you were very close to the person who has died and your child is asking difficult questions about the death, this may be very hard for you. If this is the case, find a person who is comfortable answering these questions and who the child knows well. You can then teach the child to go to this adult with these sorts of difficult questions.

CULTURAL AND RELIGIOUS BELIEFS

Each and every family and the members within it will have their own personal, cultural, spiritual and/or religious beliefs about death.

A key element to managing grief effectively is the level of support and guidance the individual receives. This support and guidance comes in many different forms: from family and friends, community networks and the individual's own spiritual and religious beliefs.

As a family, share with your child your views on what happens once we have died, but be aware of the level of understanding that your child has. For most children with SEND, they need information to be presented in a very clear manner. Think about the developmental level your child is at (see pages 8-14). If their understanding is at a very literal level, the concept of an afterlife or heaven may be hard for them to grasp and could cause confusion or concern for them. When appropriate we could say something like:

> *"Do you remember I told you Benjamin was very ill and he died? I believe when we die, we go to a place called heaven. Not everyone believes this and it's impossible for us to really know until we've died. Heaven isn't somewhere we can visit, so we cannot go and see Benjamin."*

SUPPORTING UNDERSTANDING WITH WIDER CONVERSATIONS ABOUT DEATH

Death is a difficult concept for any child to understand. All children benefit from having a wide range of conversations about what it means to die, what defines being alive and dead and the fact that once dead, that person or thing cannot live again.

The world around us provides many wonderful opportunities to discuss these concepts and develop childrens' understanding of life and death.

For example:

- **The changing of the seasons**
- **The signs of life in a tree during spring**
- **The fact that once a tree is uprooted it can no longer stay alive and will slowly die**
- **Comparing insects flying around in summer with those tangled in a spider's web**

By observing and commenting on these situations, you gradually build your child's knowledge and experiences of what it means to be alive and how and why all living things die.

Using the correct language when talking to your child is essential. We must use the words alive, living, dying, dead, death.

Be mindful of using the word 'dead' inaccurately, e.g. how often do we say things like *'my mobile has died?'* when really it has stopped working. It has not gone forever; it can be 'brought back to life' by charging it. Although these are simple, offhand comments, they can cause confusion to a child with SEND. (See page 64 and our website **winstonswish.org** for a range of activities that help build a child's understanding of alive and dead).

SAYING GOODBYE

Often families' immediate thoughts regarding funerals and other goodbye rituals are that young children and children with SEND should not attend such occasions.

A child with SEND should not be automatically left out of attending funerals or memorial services. Instead, think through the needs of your child and the nature in which the service is taking place.

Children who have experienced the death of a significant person need to be involved in some sort of 'goodbye' ceremony. Attending such an event helps them to come to terms with the death and begin to think about and understand a world without this person.

As a family, think about whether the funeral/memorial service is being held in a manner that makes it accessible and appropriate for your child's needs. That is, in terms of access, sensory needs, medical requirements etc. If it is, ask your child (in a mode of communication that is appropriate to them) whether they would like to go.

If it is not appropriate for your child to attend the funeral, it is crucial for them to have some sort of opportunity to say their own goodbye.

When Charlie's uncle died we decided it wasn't appropriate to take him to the funeral as it was such a long way away – it would have been hard to manage his medical needs. Charlie was very close to his uncle, so because he couldn't attend the funeral we had a special goodbye in the garden. We sat under a tree, the tree Charlie and his uncle used as a wicket when playing cricket together, and we talked about how we loved and missed Uncle Tim as we made a mosaic plaque with his name on it. When the memorial plaque was finished, we placed it on the tree.

FUNERALS, BURIALS AND CREMATIONS

Your child will inevitably hear the funeral, burial, cremation etc. being discussed, so it is important that these concepts are explained to them in terms they understand. The unknown nature of these events will be far more distressing than being given a basic explanation of what they are.

SEEING THE BODY

For some children (if they were very close to the person who has died), seeing the dead body may be appropriate but this is something that needs very careful consideration and detailed preparation. It is advisable for you to view the body first and have your own private goodbye before taking your child. This also allows you time to gather information about the funeral home, see what the room looks like etc. You can then prepare your child for their visit, e.g. by making a social story (see page 24) about visiting the funeral home. If it is not possible for this to happen, take another adult along with you so that you have help and support for both you and your child.

For some children, seeing the body, watching to see that there is no breathing, that the skin has changed, the body is cold etc., can help them see that the body is no longer working and that the person has died. This, in turn, can greatly support their overall understanding of the death.

If you do decide to take your child to see the body, prepare social stories and other appropriate communication devices for them in advance of the visit. Talk to them about what the body will look like as well as all other aspects of the visit prior to going.

For some children, sensitively and supportively being given the opportunity to see someone after death is invaluable; it gives them an opportunity to say goodbye and helps them to understand the reality of death.

FUNERALS

If someone close to the child has died, it is very beneficial for the family to involve the child in the planning of the funeral as far as is practically possible.

TAKING A CHILD TO A FUNERAL

If you took a typically developing baby, toddler or young child to a funeral, they would not understand the service at the time but as they got older they would know (either from their own memories or being told) that they were with their family at a very important event. This will help them to feel close to their family and, like the rest of the family and friends, to have a 'relationship' with the deceased.

Many children value the opportunity to be included in a funeral or other memorial event. You will need to think carefully about the individual needs of your own child. For some children, it may be better to plan an alternative way of saying goodbye (see an example on page 43).

If you do decide to take your child to the funeral, make sure you have someone with you who is happy and able to support both you and your child.

? What is a funeral?

When someone dies we have a special service called a funeral.

People come together at a funeral to remember the person who has died.

At the funeral we think about the person who has died.

We think about their life.

We think about how much we love them.

The funeral is a way of us saying a special goodbye to the person who died.

The following examples are possible ways of explaining a funeral to your child. These social stories/scripts are available to buy with symbol support from Widgit (see page 72 for further details).

What is a funeral? An example of how to explain this to your child:

"When someone dies, we have a special service so that everyone can get together to remember them. We think about the person who has died, remembering things they did in their life and how much we love them. The funeral is also a way of us saying a special goodbye to that person."

What happens at a funeral? An example of how to explain this to your child:

".......'s body will be in a special box called a coffin. This special box has a lid on it, so we will not be able to see ......'s body. Remember ..... is dead, s/he is no longer alive, her/his body doesn't work and so s/he doesn't need it anymore.

We will go to the church/crematorium/mosque/synagogue/temple etc. and the brown wooden box (describe it as accurately as possible to prepare the child fully, showing them a picture/photo of what the coffin will look like is a good idea) – the coffin – will be brought to the front of the church/crematorium/mosque/synagogue/ temple etc. There will be lots of people at the funeral, people who knew ...... Some people will stand up and say things about........ We will listen to some lovely music and we will sing songs/hymns. People at the funeral will be very sad that ...... is no longer alive and some may cry. You may feel like crying. Whether people do or don't cry and how much they cry doesn't matter.

At the end of the funeral, ...'s body will be taken away to be buried in the churchyard/cemetery, but we will all be going to .... to have some food and a drink with all of the family and friends of ....".

or

"At the end of the funeral ....'s body will be taken away to be cremated. Someone else does this – we will all be going to .... to have some food and a drink with all of the family and friends of ....".

What is a burial? An example of how to explain this to your child:

"After the funeral service, the coffin will be taken to the church graveyard/cemetery. At the graveyard, a big hole will have been dug in the ground – this is called a grave. ......'s coffin will be slowly lowered into the grave and then it will be covered up with earth. The imam/priest/rabbi/vicar etc. will say a few words before we all leave.

Later on, when the family are ready, a special marker called a headstone will be put on ......'s grave. This will have her/his name on it so everybody knows that s/he is buried there.

Eventually grass will grow over the grave. We will be able to visit the grave sometimes so that we can remember .... and we might bring flowers, maybe.......'s favourite flowers, to put on the grave."

What is a cremation?

Deciding how to explain the cremation will need careful consideration and will depend greatly on the level of understanding of your child. It may be inappropriate to use words such as burnt or burning with some children as this can cause great distress. Children are taught about the dangers of fire, the need to keep away from it etc., so they may not understand now why someone they love is being put in such a dangerous situation.

Here is one way of explaining cremation:

"After the funeral ......'s body will go to the crematorium to be turned into soft powdery ashes. The ashes are then put into a special pot called an urn. The urn will be given to the family. Some people decide to bury the ashes in the ground and some decide to scatter the ashes somewhere that is special to the person who has died. The family don't have to decide this straight away, they can think about it later on."

VISITING THE BURIAL PLACE

For some children, visiting the burial place or the spot where ashes were scattered can be very comforting and a good way to help with the grieving process. Other children may have scary associations with a burial ground and if after careful explanation they still feel very scared, then it might be wise to wait until they are a little older and have had time to develop their understanding of what a cemetery is.

THE FUTURE

Remember, we can be affected by grief at any time and as a result of any number of reasons. In the weeks, months and years following the bereavement there will be things that remind your child of the person who has died. They may see a person who looks a bit like Aunty Jane or hear a song that she loved to sing.

Your child may become upset about something unrelated to a death, but during this period of sadness they reflect that Grandad has died and feel this is wrong and unfair. Their thoughts of Grandad may escalate the upset that they were already experiencing.

There is also the potential effect of future deaths. When your child learns that someone else has died (regardless of whether this death affects them), this may remind them of the fact that someone special in their life is no longer with them.

When any of these periods of grief occur for whatever reason, acknowledge your child's loss and their feelings.

> *It doesn't matter what brings about the feelings of grief, the effect will be the same regardless.*

Things you can say:

> *"You seem angry. Is it because you're thinking about Nanny? Shall we talk about her? I miss her so much. Missing her makes me feel angry sometimes."*

> *"I was looking at photos of Uncle Todd yesterday. It was lovely to remember our holiday together in Cornwall. Shall we look at the photos together?"*

HOW WILL IT BE FOR MY CHILD AS THEY GROW UP?

When a child with SEND is bereaved, they will probably only be able to think about the loss in terms of how it impacts their world, and this will be influenced by their developmental level of understanding. We have talked about the importance of adults explaining to the child how the death impacts them and their life. This requires openness and honesty, giving them accurate details at their level of understanding and answering their questions. By doing this we lay the foundations for them understanding more as they grow older. They will build their awareness of what being alive and dead means and as a result, they may ask for further details about how and why the person died.

Like adults, children will revisit a death at certain points in their life. This can often be at transitions such as starting a new school, having a new respite carer, moving to college etc. or key occasions that they are unable to share with their loved one, such as their birthday, going on a plane for the first time, being a bridesmaid etc.

It does not have to be a significant transition that triggers a period of reflection or grief, it could be something small. We are unable to predict when these triggers will occur. When they do take place, talk to your child about their feelings and reassure them that it is normal to feel this way, then help them to remember the person who has died in a positive way so that they can take memories of the person with them into adulthood.

BUILDING MEMORIES

Take time to talk with your child about the person who has died. Gather stories, look at photos and collect mementos. When a person dies, our relationship with them does not stop, it just changes. Show your child ways of building memories of the person who has died. (See page 58 in the schools section for a range of memory building activities).

ANNIVERSARIES

Following a death, key dates such as the person's birthday, the anniversary of the death, Christmas etc. will often be very difficult. Acknowledge that this will probably be the case and accept that this is a normal part of grieving and will apply to your child with SEND too.

With the passing of time significant dates can help grieving children to focus on happy memories with their loved one.

HOW THE WIDER FAMILY CAN SUPPORT

It is important that your wider family and friends understand how to talk to and support your child with SEND with their bereavement. Make sure they understand that it is OK to speak to them about their loss. Explain that it is important for your child to be able to express their feelings. Demonstrate how you do this, including how you use any communication aids or resources.

Involving your wider family not only shows your child that it is not just them thinking about the death, it also shows them that it is OK to talk about it. The support of your family also helps to lessen the emotional load on you.

WHAT SCHOOLS WANT TO KNOW

SUPPORT FOR SCHOOLS COPING WITH LOSS

70% of schools have a child on roll who has been bereaved of someone important to them in the last two years.

Source: Child bereavement in Humberside educational research by Holland, J (1993).

All schools will be affected by bereavement at some point, and although there is currently no verified data, many special schools report they experience a higher frequency of pupil deaths than mainstream schools.

Never underestimate the immense impact the death of a pupil (member of staff or anyone close to the school) will have on a school community.

As a school you will encounter many different types of bereavements:

• **Children for whom a family member (or close friend) has died**

• **The death of a member of the school community (pupil or staff)**

• **Pupils who have experienced the death of a pet**

Whether it is a death that affects one child or the entire school, you need to give careful consideration to the support that you give to bereaved children.

Whether expected or unexpected, a death will often turn family life upside down. As education professionals working with a bereaved child, it is important to find out what the child has experienced, been told and crucially what they understand.

Talk to the family to find out what they have said to their child about the bereavement and how they would like the school to provide support. Schools may have differing views to families as to how death should be explained to children, especially when the child has SEND. It is important to be respectful of the family's beliefs and explain how you will answer any questions the child asks at school.

The family may say they do not believe the child is affected by the bereavement or that they have not informed them of the death yet. In both of these circumstances, the child will probably have overheard conversations and picked up on the mood of their family members (see page 34) and will need appropriate support.

> *"I didn't think Milly understood what was happening, but her concerns and questions at school about her grandad showed us that she did."* Nerys (grandmother of a 13 year old with global developmental delay)

Educators are in a unique position to help bereaved children and young people. Schools may be the one constant that children have in their lives, especially following a bereavement.

WHAT DOES A SCHOOL NEED TO DO?

- **Contact the bereaved family to express the school's condolences.**

- **Talk with the bereaved family about how they would like news of the death to be shared with the school community.**

- **If the death impacts the whole school:**

  - Write a letter to all parents/carers informing them

  - Telephone vulnerable parents/carers with the news rather than having them read the news in a letter (e.g. families who are experiencing a personal bereavement or have a seriously ill child)

  - Write a short piece for the school newsletter/website (if agreed by the family)

  - If the death affected a particular class (e.g. a pupil or member of staff in that class has died), write a more detailed letter for the parents/carers of this class, outlining the support that this class will receive

  - Be careful about social media – the rise in the use of social media can mean that some parents and families are aware of the death ahead of the school informing them of it. Even if families have received news of the death in a more informal manner, it is still important for the school to share news of the death. This formal announcement will ensure people have accurate details of the death rather than rumours and possible inaccurate information

  - Make sure all relevant people have been informed of the death (e.g. all staff personnel if the death is a member of the school community – student or staff)

If your school doesn't already have a policy or procedures for bereavement, grief and loss you may want to consider introducing these. There are guidance and information documents available from **winstonswish.org/schools** that will help. They will help you to manage future bereavements.

At a time of emotional upset, it is beneficial to have a plan in place that you can follow.

A special school in Wales which sadly experienced many pupil deaths decided to have a physical object that they would display when a member of the school community had died.

The object is a beautiful metal sunflower that is hung at the entrance of the school. This symbol communicates to the school community that there has been a death. All members of the school community should already have been informed of this news but by seeing the sunflower, it ensures that everyone entering the building is aware that there has been recent sad news. If the person coming into the school hasn't been informed of the death, they can enquire at the reception office. The school decided to display the sunflower for two weeks following a death.

RETURNING TO SCHOOL

Returning to school can be a difficult step for a bereaved child. Do not let there be an elephant in the room – something that everyone knows about but nobody discusses.

Either prior to or when the child returns to school, arrange a time to talk to the family. Express your condolences and discuss how together you will support the bereaved child.

It is important to personally welcome the child back to school away from the other children, and in doing so acknowledge the loss that has occurred.

You may say something like:

"I'm so sorry that your mummy has died; it must be difficult for you. I am here to help you."
or
"Daddy told me that your nanny died in hospital yesterday. I am so sorry. I know you loved helping Nanny do the gardening. Maybe we could do some gardening at school today."

School is a place where children learn but it should also be a nurturing environment. When a child first returns to school following a bereavement, learning may not be their number one priority.

> **If a child is in an emotional state, can they learn?** No, just as a child who is not in the right physical state (due to illness, hunger etc.) cannot learn, the same applies when a child is not in the right emotional state.

> **A child who is grieving first needs support, reassurance and care**

Schools need to support bereaved children in understanding what has happened and help them to adjust to a world without their loved one (see page 60). This will help the child to be in a position where they can learn.

Consider developing (in consultation with the family) a simple plan to support the child's return to school.

This plan would include:

- **how and when the student will return to school**
- **the name of the member of staff who will support the child's return, which should be someone who knows the child well**
- **the needs of the child e.g. extra considerations and arrangements in school including resource needs (such as those shown on page 70), the language they would like staff to use and access to support groups, counselling etc.**
- **dates for regular reviews with the child and their family**
- **discuss whether a referral to social services or other local support organisations is required (this will be important to consider when dealing with the death of a parent, grandparent, sibling etc. who had been helping to support and care for the child with SEND)**

CHECK YOUR PLANNING

Staff need to look at their planning to see what lessons are coming up and think about whether any may cause distress to the bereaved child.

For example, an assembly about road safety may be difficult for a recently bereaved child as the assembly covers road deaths. Even though the person didn't die due to a road traffic accident the child may reflect on the recent death and become upset. It is helpful that you are mindful about topics that might remind a child of death or someone who died. You may want to prepare them in advance, or have plans in place as to how you will support them if they are affected by the topic.

It is impossible to predict what will cause a 'grief trigger', but any activities that could cause upset are best discussed in advance with the child and their family to determine the best way to handle them.

IMPACT ON OTHER CHILDREN

When a bereaved child returns to school, you need to consider the impact that this may have on their peers.

If the bereaved family have given the necessary consent, it is usually beneficial to explain in very simple terms why the child is absent from school (do this at the time of the absence). This can help with the child's return to school as the class will already have a level of understanding as to what has been going on for their friend.

Listening to the views of the bereaved child and their family is crucial.

You may also wish to do a simple activity about loss and grief with the class before the bereaved child returns to school.

At circle time, read a children's story about a death (see page 70 for examples of books you could use). After the story has finished, pass a talking stone (or similar item) around the circle and encourage the children to say how they think the bereaved character in the story feels.

Welcome the bereaved child back to class (as you would after any pupil absence due to illness, holiday etc.) and briefly explain to the class why the child has been away. If the child wishes to share details about the death and how they are feeling, allow them to do so. It is quite common for children to want to share what they know about the death. Some staff may find this uncomfortable and worry about how the other children will cope with the news but as education

professionals, you will be able to support the other children's understanding and answer their questions or concerns.

It is very beneficial for the bereaved child to be able to talk about their situation in the supportive and caring environment of their classroom. Other children are generally very supportive in such situations, but you will need to be aware of the impact on pupils who may also be facing a difficult situation such as a family member being ill or if they themselves have a medical condition.

The class may also be made up of students with wide-ranging experiences and knowledge of death. Check in with pupils to see where they are with their understanding and support them accordingly.

IMPACT ON STAFF

Working in education is more than a job. School staff invest heavily in the lives of their students and they care deeply about their wellbeing. When a student experiences a bereavement or if a member of the school community dies, this can have an immense impact on staff. Schools need to recognise this and assist staff.

"Most years, my special school sadly experienced the death of at least one student. Coming to school and seeing an empty coat peg is gut-wrenching and having this happen time and time again takes its toll."
Sophie (a special school teacher)

How can a school help staff with student deaths?

Provide:

• opportunities to talk and share feelings

• a way for the staff to say 'goodbye' (this is especially important if staff are unable to attend the funeral)

• bereavement training

• a bereavement and grief policy/procedures

SUPPORTING FAMILIES

Families will look for differing levels of support. The family who is bereaved will probably have a tight support mechanism around them but they may also turn to the school for support.

The families of other pupils may also be affected by the death and look to the school for guidance.

- Have resources prepared that parents can use at home e.g. how to explain death to their child, the use of symbols and other AAC (see page 27).

- Have signposting to local support groups, charities and useful websites prepared and ready to hand out.

- Families tend to turn to the member of school staff that they are most familiar with to gain support and advice. Schools need to ensure staff are equipped to provide this.

- If your school has a Family Liaison Officer (FLO) and/or School Nurse (SN), these members of staff will be key in supporting families. Both the FLO and SN will be able to help disseminate information to families.

- The FLO may be able to meet with families who are bereaved, either at their home, school or a neutral environment such as a coffee shop – whatever space the family is most comfortable in.

- The SN can also help with these types of meetings and conversations. If you have both roles within your school, then the SN will probably be better placed to deal with concerns that other families have about the medical needs of their child. The death of one child can heighten parents' concerns about the health of their own child, especially if their child has a life–limiting condition.

Reassure parents that handling death and bereavement is not a natural parenting skill; it is not something that we 'know how to do' upon becoming a parent.

BUILDING MEMORIES

When a school experiences a death that affects the whole community, it is important to acknowledge the significance of the loss. A memorial service or special assembly is a good way of doing this.

> The grieving process can be delayed for a child if they are denied the opportunity to say goodbye.

THINGS TO CONSIDER WHEN ORGANISING A MEMORIAL

- Involve the pupils as much as possible. This will help them with processing the loss.

- The children can assist with choosing photos, music, songs etc.

- The students can also help to decide whether people should be asked to dress up or to wear something special for the memorial. For example, if the person loved hats, everyone could wear a hat, or if their favourite colour was blue, everyone could wear blue.

- If the person who has died was particularly known for something (e.g. a child loving Peppa Pig or a member of staff loving The Great British Bake Off), every child in the school could perhaps have a Peppa Pig or cake template to colour and decorate. These could then be made into a special display during the assembly.

- The memorial should be organised and delivered so that it is accessible to all children at the school.

- Inform the children that a memorial is going to take place. Use a photo of the person who has died to help explain this. It may also be beneficial to write a social story (see page 24) to explain what will happen at the memorial to better prepare the students.

- Do not exclude or remove any pupil who wishes to attend the memorial.

- If the memorial is for a pupil, choose examples of the child's work, favourite toys, etc. to display.

- All children (and staff) should be involved in joining in (at a level that is comfortable for the individual) with the songs and activities of the event and be given the opportunity to speak: sharing stories, recollections, memories and thoughts.

- Consider having a 'Remembering [name of the deceased] Box' – a box where thoughts and feelings about the individual who has died can be collected. This should be available during and after the assembly and for some considerable time thereafter so that children and staff can add their thoughts and feelings when they feel comfortable and able to do so. They may not have felt able to stand up and do this during the memorial or thoughts may not have come to them at that point, but it will be a very important part of their ongoing grieving process to share these things. Entries to the box can be named or anonymous. At a later date, they can all be collated and shared with the whole school along with the family of the deceased person.

ANNIVERSARIES

Be prepared for significant dates: the anniversary of the death, the person's birthday, Mothering Sunday (for a child whose mother has died) etc. Although 'grief triggers' can occur at any time, key dates can often be a time when bereaved children are in particular need of support and reassurance. Prior to these dates, talk to the family about what they will be doing and how they would like school to support this.

It is generally best to acknowledge the date rather than avoid it.

"It was Father's Day shortly after my husband died. Nathan's school was brilliant, they talked to me about the activities they would be doing in school and asked if Nathan could bring a photo of his dad in so that he could make a special 'I love my dad' photo frame. He also made lovely cards for his two grandfathers".
Josie (mum of a 9 year old with autism)

As a school you may wish to support your students' understanding of death and bereavement by taking part in one of our annual fundraising events. These events are a great way to start conversations about grief and a wonderful way to support the work Winston's Wish does with schools up and down the country, ensuring bereaved children get access to support when they need it.

For further details visit **winstonswish.org/get-involved/schools/** or contact the Winston's Wish community fundraising team.

ACTIVITIES TO HELP SUPPORT A BEREAVED CHILD WITH SEND

Try to provide the child with a range of different types of activities:

- Physical activities – that allow them to release their emotions physically

- Reassurance activities – that show the child they are OK and that not everyone they know and love is suddenly going to die

- Comforting activities – providing comfort to the physical symptoms of grief

- Therapeutic/holistic activities – the use of the arts and alternative approaches

- Remembering activities – creating memories about the person who died

- Activities to develop understanding – of death and grief

Here are a couple of examples for each of the different types of activities. For further activity ideas, visit our website **winstonswish.org**

PHYSICAL ACTIVITIES

Providing grieving children with physical outlets is an excellent way to give them a temporary release from the grieving process. It allows them to 'get away' from the deep feelings of bereavement. Physical activities also support the grieving process. While engaged in the physical task, they will be able to release emotions physically and this can lead to emotions being expressed verbally or through AAC (including body language which will be especially important for children who are non–verbal).

- throwing balls, beanbags etc. randomly or into/at targets

- manipulating/pounding clay or playdough

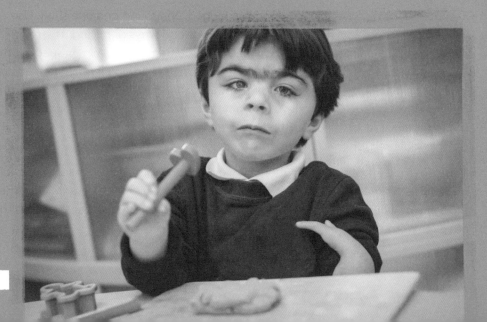

REASSURANCE ACTIVITIES

• If the child is able to, get them to tell you their top five worries and then together talk through these worries. (There is a pre-made set of worry cards in the Widgit Bereavement and Loss Symbol Resources Set, see page 72).

• Make friendship bracelets for each other, so the bereaved child can see on their wrist the number of friends and family that they still have around them. By making the friendship bracelet with a range of interesting materials, it is also a comforting multisensory resource which they will be able to explore and feel.

• Create a special bag that the child can access at any time which has a range of things in it to help them smile (things that they typically enjoy e.g. bubbles, silly putty, twiddle toy, favourite music to listen to etc.)

• Have a hot water bottle or furry toy that they can cuddle in times of sadness or distress, including if they are experiencing somatic complaints such as a sore tummy, headaches or just generally not feeling well. Somatic complaints are when unexpressed feelings and emotions can lead to physical symptoms or discomfort.

THERAPEUTIC/HOLISTIC ACTIVITIES

• Emotion stones – have three stones: one jagged, one round and one shiny. Use these three stones to express different emotions and ways of feeling. The round stone = normal everyday feelings, jagged = difficult emotions, shiny = special times. Ask the children to choose the stone that they are feeling and if possible to express why they are feeling this way. Even if the child is unable to verbalise how they are feeling, selecting the stone relevant to how they are feeling allows them to share their emotions. Also, the opportunity to handle and explore the stone can often be an enjoyable sensory and therapeutic activity for the child.

• Music therapy is not only educational, enjoyable and relaxing for children, but it also allows them to be expressive in a different way. It allows them to release their thoughts and emotions about the death in a musical manner rather than with the need for words.

REMEMBERING ACTIVITIES

• Use objects related to the individual who has died (e.g. an item of their clothing, a favourite toy or book etc.) to help the child talk about the person and share how they are feeling.

• Laminate photos of the person who has died so that the children can have them in their bag, classroom tray, locker, at home etc. They will then be able to look at them whenever they need to.

FOR DEATHS THAT AFFECT THE SCHOOL COMMUNITY

• Create a 'stone pile' – every time you share a memory of the person that died, add a stone to a decorative bowl. You could write a few words on each stone. This activity could also be done by adding leaves to a decorative tree, flowers into a wall display about a garden or whatever other imagery fits for the person who has died and supports the grieving children's relationship with them.

• Choose an activity/routine that the class really identified with the person who has died, e.g. playing a certain game, laying the table for snack time (as this was the child's favourite job to do in class) etc. As you lead this activity, intentionally talk about the person who has died and how they used to do this task. It can often be much easier to talk about a person who has died when you are actively engaged in doing something that they enjoyed.

ACTIVITIES TO DEVELOP AN UNDERSTANDING OF DEATH AND GRIEF

• Have a vase of flowers and watch them gradually wilt and die, then compare these flowers to a vase of living flowers. The child will see that the dead flowers will not come back to life, however much water and sunlight is given to them.

• Help to develop the child's understanding of the range of emotions we can experience by using a mirror and photographs of people displaying different emotions. Talk with the child about what you think the person in the photo is doing and how and why they may feel the way they do. You can also practise making the different faces in the mirror with the child.

A CURRICULUM TO SUPPORT THE ISSUES OF BEREAVEMENT AND GRIEF

Children are never too young to talk about life and death.

- **The tree that has died in the playground**
- **The chicks that have hatched**
- **Seeing the cut flowers change over time from a beautiful bouquet to dead flowers**
- **The birth of a baby brother**
- **A badger on the side of the road**

Schools should consider having a curriculum that embeds the teaching of life, death and loss across its subjects and across all year groups. Children need to develop an understanding of what life and death are before they can accept and manage their own feelings of loss and grief.

Having a curriculum that covers life and death will not only build the students' understanding of what it means to be alive and dead but it will also help them to cope with bereavements when they occur.

Here are a couple of examples for each of the different subject areas. For further curriculum ideas visit our website **winstonswish.org.**

With all of these examples it is important that the information is presented at the child's developmental level of understanding (see page 8), using their preferred mode(s) of communication (see page 26).

PSHE (PERSONAL, SOCIAL, HEALTH AND ECONOMIC)

- When learning about our body and how it works, emphasise what the key signs of life are and that when these are no longer present, a person is no longer living; they are dead.

- Teach what different emotions look and feel like, including the physical impact they can have on our body, e.g. when we cry a lot, we can get very hot and tired.

PE

- During PE lessons talk about the breath and heart rate. When the children experience their heart rate increasing, ask them to put their hand on their chest to feel their heart beating and when they feel out of breath to put their hand in front of their mouth to feel the movement of air. Explain that all of these things mean we are alive. When someone has died, they stop breathing, their heart stops, and they are no longer alive.

ENGLISH

- When reading works of fiction and non-fiction and someone or something (animal, plant etc.) dies, do not gloss over this. Use it is as a discussion point for what alive and dead are. Reinforce that when someone dies they cannot be brought back. Stories that talk of monsters coming back to life are just that – stories, fiction, make-believe, and children need to know that this cannot happen when a person dies in real life.

- Explore the language of death, grief and loss – look at condolence cards, death announcements in newspapers etc. Make a list of the different words and phrases that are used and think about whether we feel these are the best words to use. If euphemisms are used in the cards, make it clear to the children what these really mean and come up with your own simpler and clearer phrases.

SCIENCE

- When learning about the life cycles of animals, insects and plants etc. look at and discuss what they each look like and how they behave when they are alive and also when they are dead.

- Build on the PE lessons (mentioned on page 64) by learning how our bodies work, what they look and feel like when they are working well, what happens when they are not working so well and include when we are ill and need help from doctors, nurses and hospitals etc. Sensitively reference that sometimes ill health or an accident can mean that a person's body is 'so badly damaged' to a point that even though the doctors and nurses do all that they can to help, they are sometimes unable to make the person better and they sadly die.

HISTORY

- When different historical figures are covered in history lessons, you can also talk about how and when they died so that children realise that these 'big names in history' do not have super powers that allow them to go on living forever; they are humans just like us.

As well as having planned lessons that cover life, death and grief, school staff can also make the most of any incidental learning opportunities that arise.

> When a child comes into school and says they have a new baby cousin.

> When a student tells us that their favourite character in a TV show has been killed.

> When there is a natural disaster in the news.

Key things that a bereaved child needs:

- To know that they are safe and that there are people who care for them
- To have their questions answered
- Security, affection and reassurance
- Opportunities to talk in their own time
- Opportunities to be left alone
- To be given the opportunity/a way to say 'goodbye'
- To be given help to understand about the death
- Help to manage this immense change in their life
- Ways to remember the person
- Continued support and awareness: in the days, weeks, months and years that follow a death

SHARING INFORMATION

There is no time limit to grief – we do not get over a loss, instead we learn to live with it.

It is important for schools to remember that a bereaved child doesn't stop being a bereaved child at the end of an academic year. Make sure the relevant details of the child's bereavement are passed on to their next teacher and support team, which needs to be the case at the end of each and every year.

SIGNS THAT THE BEREAVED CHILD MAY NEED FURTHER SUPPORT

You do not need to be a trained counsellor or mental health professional to help the bereaved children that you work with. The education professionals of a grieving child will know that child incredibly well and will generally be able to help and support them with their grief, but we must be open and prepared to seeing when the child may require further professional support.

As the teacher/teaching assistant/key worker etc., you can assist a great deal, but some children may require the additional specialist assistance of a doctor, counsellor, psychologist or psychiatrist. If they do, this in no way means that you have failed them. The support you have given them and the work that you have done will have all been beneficial but they now need a little extra guidance.

The following are things to look out for:

• they refuse to acknowledge that the person has died – even after detailed support and teaching about the death

• they act as if nothing has changed (not just in the short term, but for a significant period of time)

• they start to suffer panic attacks

• they are harming themselves or others

• they become withdrawn (or are more so than normal)

• they talk about or threaten suicide

• they become involved in extreme anti–social behaviour

• they start to use drugs or alcohol

If you become aware of a child or young person doing any of these things, you need to talk to their parents immediately so that a referral to another professional, such as a doctor, counsellor, psychologist or psychiatrist, can be made.

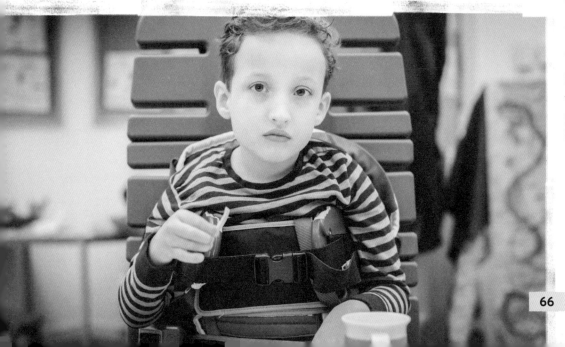

67

GLOSSARY

AAC	**Augmentative and Alternative Communication** is the term used to describe a range of methods that support speech and communication.
ASD	**Autism spectrum disorder** is a lifelong, developmental disability that affects how a person communicates with and relates to other people, and how they experience the world around them.
Comic strip	A basic representation of a situation made using simple conversation drawings and stick figures. Colour can also be added to the words in the comic strip to help represent the emotional content of the statements.
Communication aid	A **communication aid** helps an individual to communicate more effectively with the people around them.
CP	**Cerebral palsy** is a group of permanent movement disorders that appear in early childhood. Signs and symptoms vary among people and over time. Symptoms include poor coordination, stiff muscles, weak muscles, and tremors. There may also be problems with sensation, vision, hearing, swallowing and speech.
DS	**Down's syndrome** is a genetic disorder caused by the presence of all or part of a third copy of chromosome 21. It is typically associated with physical growth delays, mild to moderate intellectual disability, and characteristic facial features.
Dyslexia	A learning difficulty that can cause problems with reading, writing and spelling. It's a specific learning difficulty, which means it causes problems with certain abilities used for learning, such as reading and writing.

Euphemisms	A word or expression used in place of one that may be found difficult, offensive or suggest something unpleasant.
Eye gaze	**Eye gaze** or eye tracking is a way of accessing a computer or communication aid using a mouse that you control with your eyes.
FLO	A **Family Liaison Officer** is a role found in many schools. The FLO is a point of contact and support for parents and children if they have any concerns, issues, worries or feedback they wish to raise or discuss with the school.
GDD	**Global developmental delay** is an umbrella term used when children are significantly delayed in their cognitive and physical development.
High-tech AAC	Communication aids that rely on computer technology.
Intensive Interaction	An approach that teaches the pre-speech fundamentals of communication for individuals who have severe learning difficulties and/or autism and who are still at the early stage of communication development.
LD	A **learning disability** affects the way a person understands information and how they communicate. A LD can be mild, moderate or severe.
Low-tech AAC	Using pictures and symbols to support communication.
No-tech AAC	Using gestures, pointing and body language to support communication.
Non-verbal	An individual who is without verbal language and it is not thought that they will develop verbal skills.
Objects of reference	**Objects of reference** are objects that are systematically and consistently used with a person to represent people, places, objects and activities. They are used alongside the spoken word.

PD	A **physical disability** is a limitation on a person's physical functioning, mobility, dexterity or stamina.
PECS	**Picture Exchange Communication System** is an approach that develops early expressive communication skills using pictures/symbols. It is a functional communication system that develops important communication and social skills.
Pet therapy	**Pet therapy** builds on the bond between humans and animals. Interacting with a friendly pet may help many physical and mental issues.
PMLD	A **profound and multiple learning disability** is when an individual has a severe learning disability plus other disabilities that significantly affect their ability to communicate and be independent.
PODD books	**Pragmatic Organisation Dynamic Display** communication books are a means of communicating using a structured book (that contains symbols and words) and technique. PODD books can be paper based or an electronic version on a tablet.
Pre-verbal	An individual who is currently without verbal language, but is developing the ability to communicate verbally.
PSHE	**Personal, Social, Health and Economic Education** is a curriculum subject which focuses on developing children's knowledge, skills and attributes to help keep them healthy and safe, and to prepare them for life beyond school.
SEND	**Special Educational Needs** is defined as a learning difficulty or disability that makes learning a challenge for a child.
Separation anxiety	Resulting from the separation or the threat of separation from a main carer.

Sign language	A system of communicating using visual gestures and signs. There are many different types of sign language. Makaton and Signalong are the most popular ones used with children with SEND.
SLD	Children with **severe learning difficulties** have very significant cognitive impairments.
SN	**School Nurse** – some schools have a SN permanently on site to help support students medical needs.
Social story	Social stories are short descriptions of a particular situation, event or activity, which include specific information about what to expect in that situation and why. Social stories often include pictures/photos/symbols.
Somatic	Unexpressed feelings and emotions which lead to physical complaints symptoms or discomfort such as headaches, stomach pains, lethargy etc.
Switches	**Switches** come in a range of formats, sizes and levels of complexity. A BIGmack (and the smaller version LITTLEmack) is a battery operated switch that allows you to record any sound onto it and then when the user presses the switch the sound is played. Jelly switches allow individuals with physical and/or cognitive difficulties to access a computer. Some switches enable the child to operate standard mouse functions such as click, right-click and double-click. Others can be configured to operate any mouse or keyboard input.
Symbols	**Symbols** provide a visual representation of a word or concept. They are images which are used to support text, making the meaning clearer and easier to understand.
Tablets	A **tablet** computer is a mobile device, typically with a mobile operating system and touch screen display. Some children with SEND use a communication app on a tablet to help them express themselves.
Weighted blanket	A **weighted blanket** provides firm, deep pressure which can provide comfort and support for an individual.

BOOKS AND RESOURCES

A JUMBLE OF KNOTTED THOUGHTS

By Sarah Helton

A sensory story to support bereavement and grief.
Available from www.backpocketteacher.co.uk

A POCKET FULL OF PLASTERS

Winston's Wish

Difficult days are not predictable. Sometimes a painful memory is suddenly recalled during a maths lesson, or waiting for the bus. These 10 'plasters' of advice are shared by young people as things that have helped them in these situations. The subtle design means the plasters can be unravelled and read without prying eyes from friends spotting anything out of the ordinary.

A SPECIAL KIND OF GRIEF

By Sarah Helton

A guide for supporting bereavement and loss in special schools (and other SEND settings).
Published by Jessica Kingsley Publishers
Available from www.jkp.com

IS DADDY COMING BACK IN A MINUTE?

By Elke Barber and Alex Barber

A true story about Alex, the death of his daddy, and how his mum helped him to understand what dead means. This story helps to explain sudden death.

MEMORY BOX

Winston's Wish

Children need help to build and hold on to positive memories. It is a good idea to collect and keep special things connected with the person who has died in a safe box, like this memory box. The items collected can be used to prompt memories and meaningful stories that will mean a lot to the child in the future. Available in different designs.

MISSING MUMMY

By Rebecca Cobb

A book that deals with the loss of a parent from a child's point of view and explores the many emotions a bereaved child may experience, from anger to guilt and from sadness to bewilderment. The book also focuses on the positive – the recognition that the child is still part of a family, and that his memories of his mother are to be treasured.

MUDDLES PUDDLES AND SUNSHINE: YOUR ACTIVITY BOOK WHEN SOMEONE HAS DIED

By Diana Crossley – a Winston's Wish publication

This activity book offers practical and sensitive support for children under 11 and is designed to be completed by a child working with a caring adult.

LITTLE BOX OF BIG THOUGHTS

Winston's Wish

Each box contains a variety of cards – some are simply blank, others have helpful prompts like 'I love you because...' and 'A favourite memory I have is...'. A simple yet remarkably effective way to create meaningful memories of important relationships. It becomes a lasting legacy of a parent's thoughts.

REMEMBERING LUCY

By Sarah Helton

A children's story book about grief and bereavement in a school.
Published by Jessica Kingsley Publishers
Available from www.jkp.com

SAD

By Michael Rosen and illustrated by Quentin Blake

A powerful illustrated book that vividly illustrates a father's grief.

WHEN DINOSAURS DIE: A GUIDE TO UNDERSTANDING DEATH

By Laurie Krasny Brown and Mark Brown

This factual picture book uses cartoon dinosaurs to illustrate the text and comment on what is said. It is a bright and colourful book that explains death in a simple and unthreatening way. It covers many issues including 'why does someone die?', 'feelings about death' and 'saying goodbye'.

WIDGIT BEREAVEMENT AND LOSS SYMBOL RESOURCE SET

By Sarah Helton

A set of resources designed for children, young people and their families to help them through the process of bereavement and loss.
Available from www.widgit.com

USEFUL WEBSITES

BackPocketTeacher
SEND advice, resources and training for parents and professionals, specialising in bereavement, grief and loss.
www.backpocketteacher.co.uk

Inclusive Technology
Supplier of software and hardware for people with SEND.
www.inclusive.co.uk

Intensive Interaction Institute
The institute defines, develops and disseminates the theory and practice of Intensive Interaction.
www.intensiveinteraction.org

Makaton
A language programme using signs and symbols to help people to communicate. It is designed to support spoken language and the signs and symbols are used with speech, in spoken word order.
www.makaton.org

Sensory Directory
Resources for children with SEND.
www.sensorydirect.com

Signalong
A key word sign-supported communication system based on British Sign Language and is used in spoken word order. It uses speech, sign, body language, facial expression and voice tone to reference the link between sign and word.
www.signalong.org.uk

TTS
Supplier of teaching resources including resources for children with SEND.
www.tts-group.co.uk

Widgit
Widgit symbols aid communication. They are simply drawn, colourful symbols which illustrate a single concept in a clear and concise way.
www.widgit.com

WHERE TO SEEK FURTHER SUPPORT
BEREAVEMENT SUPPORT

Childhood Bereavement Network
Provides a directory of organisations around the country that can offer local bereavement services to families and young people. Also offers publications, information and training.
Phone: 020 7843 6309
Email: cbn@ncb.org.uk
www.childhoodbereavementnetwork.org.uk

Winston's Wish
Winston's Wish offers guidance, information and support to those caring for a bereaved child through a Freephone National Helpline and a range of publications and resources (including memory boxes).
Freephone National Helpline: 08088 020021
Email: ask@winstonswish.org
www.winstonswish.org

SEND SUPPORT

Action on Hearing Loss (formerly RNID)
The UK's leading charity supporting people with hearing loss, deafness and tinnitus.
Phone: 0808 808 0123
Textphone: 0808 808 9000
SMS: 0780 0000 360
Email: information@hearingloss.org.uk
www.actiononhearingloss.org.uk

BILD (The British Institute of Learning Disabilities)
Phone: 0121 415 6960
Email: enquiries@bild.org.uk
www.bild.org.uk

British Dyslexia Association

The BDA is the voice of dyslexic people. They aim to influence government and other institutions to promote a dyslexia friendly society, that enables dyslexic people of all ages to reach their full potential.

Phone: 0333 405 4555

Email: helpline@bdadyslexia.org.uk

www.bdadyslexia.org.uk

Down's Syndrome Association

Information and support for families and professionals.

Phone: 0333 1212 300

Email: info@downs–syndrome.org.uk

www.downs–syndrome.org.uk

MENCAP

The Learning Disability Charity – working with children and adults with a learning disability and their families and carers to improve their lives and opportunities.

Phone: 0808 808 1111

Email: community@mencap.org.uk

www.mencap.org.uk

Mind

Mind is the leading mental health charity in England and Wales and works for a better life for everyone with experience of mental distress. Local groups offer supported housing, counselling, befriending, advocacy, employment and training services etc.

Phone: 020 8519 2122

Email: supporterrelations@mind.org.uk

www.mind.org.uk

NASEN (The National Association for Special Educational Needs)

Phone: 01827 311500

Email: welcome@nasen.org.uk

www.nasen.org.uk

National Autistic Society

The UK's leading charity for autistic people and their families. The goal of NAS is to help transform lives, change attitudes and create a society that works for autistic people.

Phone: 020 7833 2299

Email: nas@nas.org.uk

www.autism.org.uk

PAMIS (Promoting A More Inclusive Society)

PAMIS support people with profound and multiple learning disabilities – their families, carers and professionals.

Phone: 0141 572 0782

Email: tayside@pamis.org.uk

www.pamis.org.uk

Pets as Therapy

Pets as Therapy seeks to enhance health and wellbeing in the community through visits of trusted volunteers with their behaviourally assessed animals. It provides a visiting service in hospitals, hospices, nursing and care homes, special needs schools and a variety of other venues all across the UK.

www.petsastherapy.org

RNIB

The Royal National Institute of Blind People is a UK charity offering information, support and advice to almost two million people in the UK with sight loss.

Phone: 0303 123 9999

Email: helpline@rnib.org.uk

www.rnib.org.uk

SCOPE

The disability equality charity in England and Wales. SCOPE provides practical information and emotional support and campaigns for a fairer society.

Phone: 0808 800 3333

Email: helpline@scope.org.uk

www.scope.org.uk

Sense

Sense supports people with complex disabilities, including those who are deafblind.

Phone: 0300 330 9256

Email: info@sense.org.uk

www.sense.org.uk

74